The Basketball Pass Cut Catch Guide

by Sidney Goldstein

author of **The Basketball Coach's Bible**

and **The Basketball Player's Bible**

GOLDEN AURA PUBLISHING

The Nitty-Gritty Basketball Series

The Basketball Pass Cut Catch Guide
by Sidney Goldstein

Published by:

GOLDEN AURA PUBLISHING

Post Office Box 41012

Philadelphia, PA 19127 U.S.A.

Second Edition Copyright © 1999 by Sidney Goldstein

Printed in the U.S.A.

Library of Congress Card Number   98- 75671

Goldstein, Sidney

The Basketball Pass Cut Catch Guide

Sidney Goldstein.--Second Edition, 1999

Basketball-Coaching

ISBN 1-884357-34-2

Softcover

Contents

Introduction

Over many years of coaching, planning, and studying, I found ways to teach each and every skill even to the most unskilled player. This scheme of learning did not come from any book. I tried things in practice. I modified them till they worked. Even players who could not simultaneously chew bubble gum and walk learned the skills. This booklet, part of **The Nitty-Gritty Basketball Series**, is one result of this effort. I believe you can benefit from my work.

Who Can Use This Information

This booklet is the perfect tool for anybody who wants to coach, teach, and/or learn basketball:

- A parent who wants to teach his or her child
- A player who wants to understand and play the game better
- A little league or recreation league coach
- A high school or junior high school coach
- A college coach, a professional coach
- A women's or a men's coach

This booklet contains material from **The Basketball Player's Bible**. Chapter 1 gives the keys to learning the skills presented. I present the skills in lesson form. Chapter 2 gives the features of each lesson. The largest chapter, Chapter 3, presents the lessons in order. Check the **Lessons Needed Before** feature as you progress.

The Basketball Player's Bible contains the lessons presented here and many other related ones.

Golden Aura's Nitty-Gritty Basketball Series
by Sidney Goldstein

See the description in the back of this book.

The Basketball Coach's Bible

The Basketball Player's Bible

The Basketball Shooting Guide

The Basketball Scoring Guide

The Basketball Dribbling Guide

The Basketball Defense Guide

The Basketball Pass Cut Catch Guide

Basketball Fundamentals

Planning Basketball Practice

Videos for the Guides soon available

HOW TO CONTACT THE AUTHOR

The author seeks your comments about this book. Sidney Goldstein is available for consultation and clinics with coaches and players. Contact him at:

Golden Aura Publishing
PO Box 41012
Philadelphia, PA 19127
215 438-4459

Chapter One

1

Principles of Learning

How To Use The Pass Cut Catch Guide

Start from the beginning and progress through the lessons one by one. Typically, I arrange them in order of increasing difficulty. You may want to skip some topics. However, use the **Lessons Needed Before** feature to insure that you do not omit needed techniques.

The most important as well as the most frequently skipped lessons involve techniques. If you spend the needed time on these lessons, you will improve exponentially on a daily basis. Skip them and improvement may be delayed for months and even years.

One big misconception about learning the basics is that to improve you must practice things millions of times. I've tried it and so has everybody else. It does not work well. Volume of practice does not necessarily bring about improvement; practicing properly insures improvement. The following **principles** tell you what and how to practice. A list of **Counterproductive Beliefs** follows. These often widely held ideas prevent learning because they do not work.

The Principles of Pass Catch Cut

These skills are so interrelated that I present the principles in one section.

1. Passing technique starts with touch and wrist movement as well as arm position. Most passes involve a flick of the wrist with little arm movement. See Lesson 1.

2. Faking is an important part of cutting technique. See Lessons 16.

3. Passing as well as catching involves pivoting.

4. Use the overhead, side, and bounce pass to avoid the defense. See lessons 2-4.

5. Bounce passes, which are especially effective in traffic, need to be carefully timed. See Lesson 4.

6. Baseball passes are good for long passes. See Lesson 5 and 6.

7. Communication is necessary to insure that the ball and the cutter meet at a point. See Lesson 8.

8. Realistic passing lessons need defense. See Lessons 9 and 19.

9. Front and back weaves are a good way to practice timing without defense in a game-like situation.

10. The footwork involved in catching a pass is tricky–jump, catch, step one, two. Lessons 11 and 13 cover this.

11. You must catch passes before you stop running forward. See lessons 12 and 13.

12. You must step in front of your opponent before going for a loose ball. See Lesson 14.

13. You must attempt to catch all passes, even if the pass is off the mark. See Lesson 15.

14. The key to catching passes and to team offense involves faking and cutting to the ball or open area. Lessons 11 and 12 cover this.

15. The last part of a cut is a jump for the ball. Another way to say this is to always jump to the ball before you catch it. See Lesson 13.

Counterproductive Beliefs

1. Good plays are the key to team offense. Nope. Players need to learn the fundamentals of offense. The greatest plays ever dreamed cannot work if players do not cut or communicate well. The worst plays ever conceived will work if players know how to cut, pass, and communicate.

2. Chest passes may have historical significance but they are worthless with defense. Holding the ball close to the body at waist height is a terrible place to have the ball. You can't pass fake, ball fake or readily reach around the offense. Neither can you fake a shot with the ball in this position. Say good-bye to this pass and use more effective ones.

3. It is easy to catch a ball. No–the footwork is quite difficult. The hands need to be in the proper position as well. I see pros and college players routinely drop passes because their hands are not clawed with fingers spread.

4. Timing between players just develops. If you can wait for evolution to take place I bet it will. However, if you practice timing it will develop within days rather than eons.

5. Passing is an easy skill. Passing as well as cutting may even be more difficult to learn than shooting or dribbling. Their are several reasons for this. One, timing between the passer and cutter is involved. Two, flicking passes is rarely taught, and it is not that easy to do. Adding defense on the passer and or catcher makes passing very difficult. Lesson 19 demonstrates just how difficult.

Chapter Two

2

Lesson Features

Table Information

At a glance this table gives an overview to aid in planning. It supplies the name and number of each lesson as well as these additional features: lessons needed before, the number of players needed, the effort level, the estimated practice times, whether you need a ball and/or a court. Practice the *no ball* or *no court* lessons for homework while watching TV or sitting down. The Player's Corner section of each lesson supplies some of the same information.

Number

The lessons are numbered in order from easiest to hardest, from most fundamental to most complicated. Typically, do them in order. Sometimes you can skip. If you do, check the **Lessons Needed Before** feature so that you do not skip essential lessons.

Name

A name related to each lesson serves as a descriptive mnemonic device (I almost forgot that). When skills are executed simultaneously, their names are directly coupled like Pivot Around Shoot or Jump Hook. Lessons with skills separately performed are named, for example, Pivot with Defense, where one player pivots on offense while the other is on defense.

Brief

In one sentence (usually) the **brief** immediately familiarizes you with the lesson by stating the action and movement involved.

Why Do This

When do you use this in a game? What is the significance of the lesson? What fundamentals do you practice? How does this lesson relate to others? The **Why Do This** section answers these questions.

Directions

These are step-by-step directions for you.

Key Points

This feature emphasizes important points in the directions so that you will not make common mistakes.

When You Are More Expert

These more expert lessons usually add another step, combine another skill, or change one variable in the previous lesson. Some lessons have as many as four expert additions.

Player's Corner and Section Tables

At a glance you can see that the **Player's Corner** lists 8 useful pieces of information about each lesson. The **Table of Lessons** in **Appendix C** and each **Section Table** contain this same information. **Xs** in the tables mean <u>yes</u>. Dashes (-) mean <u>no</u>.

• Lessons Needed Before

Do these lessons before this current one. If you don't, then you will have a problem. Often you can skip lessons without it being disastrous. Not so with the lessons listed as Lessons Needed Before.

• Additional Needs

This feature gives 4 useful pieces of information.

Ball and Court

For most lessons you need a **ball** and a **court**. However, for some either one or the other or both are not needed. These lessons can be practiced at home while watching TV or in your backyard. **Xs** in the tables mean <u>yes</u>.

Players

Most lessons are for individuals. So, the Player's Corner lists additional players needed, whereas the Tables give the total number (which is always one more than additional players).

Assist

For some lessons you need an inactive **assistant** to either act as a dummy player or more importantly to closely watch what you are doing. **Xs** in the tables mean <u>yes</u>.

• Effort or Effort Level

The effort level of a lesson involves the physical effort involved. Level 1 lessons involve technique. Do them slowly;

they often do not resemble the skill performed in a game because 2 to 5 technique lessons often comprise a skill. In situations calling for defense, the defense expends little effort.

Level 2 lessons are at the practice level. Any skill practiced at a moderate pace like shooting or pivoting is at level 2. This level is a catchall for lessons between levels 1 and 3. Defense against offense makes a moderate effort.

Level 3 lessons are at the game level. Players sprint and perform at maximum effort. Pressure is on players. Offense and defense go full speed against each other. Games are easy compared to these lessons.

• Daily Practice Time

This is a time range needed to practice this lesson. Note that many lessons have additional parts. These will take more time.

• More Expert Lessons

Each of these additions adds one or two parameters to the main lesson. Few are optional. Most need to be done after you are more expert.

FEATURES OF THE DIAGRAMS

Lines and Arrows

Solid lines indicate movement of players whereas dashed lines usually indicate movement of the ball. One exception is dashed lines used to show pivoting direction. The types of arrows used are solid for movement and hollow for passes. A different type of arrow head is used for fakes. See the diagrams.

Body Position of Player

The body of a player is shown from an overhead view two ways. The line or the ellipse represents the shoulders. The

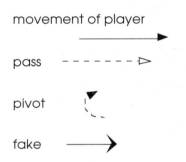

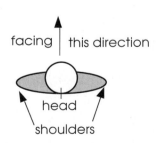

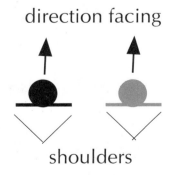

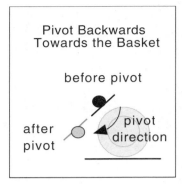

Pivot Backwards
Towards the Basket

before pivot

after pivot

pivot direction

circle shows the head. The player is always facing away from the shoulders toward the head.

Shades for Different Positions

When a player is shown in two positions in the same diagram, the first position is black and the second is lighter in color. Often offense or defense are shown in light and dark shades. In some diagrams shades are used to designate the position of a player when the ball of the same shade is in the diagramed position.

Numbers in Multistep Movements

Many drills involve multiple steps. Each step, as well, may have several timed movements that need to be executed in order. So, in the diagrams for each step, the numbers indicate the order of the movements. One (1) means first, two (2) second and so on. If two players move at the same time the numbers will be the same, so there may be several ones or twos in the diagram.

In the diagram below, there are three ones in the diagram. This indicates that these players move at the same time. There are two twos; one indicates a cut, while the other indicates a pass.

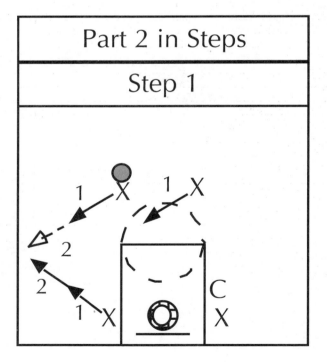

Part 2 in Steps

Step 1

Chapter Three

3

Pass Cut Catch
Lessons 1-21

L E S S O N	NAME	A S S I S T	P L A Y E R S	C O U R T	B A L L	E F F O R T	L E S S O N	Lessons Before	REF TO *Coach's Manual*	DAILY TIME	E X T R A
1-21	**PASS CUT CATCH**										
1	Passing Technique	x	1	-	-	1	**1**	none	9.0	1-2	0
2	Overhead Short Pass	-	2	-	x	1-2	**2**	1	9.1	5	0
3	Side Short Pass	-	2	-	x	1-2	**3**	2	9.11	5	0
4	Bounce Pass	-	2	-	x	1-2	**4**	3	9.12	5	0
5	Baseball Pass	-	2	x	x	2	**6**	none	9.2	5	0
6	Baseball Pass Cut	-	2	x	x	2	**7**	5	9.3	5-10	1
7	Pivot Pass	-	2	-	x	2	**8**	3, 10	9.5	5-10	1
8	Pass Communication 1-2	-	2	-	x	2	**9**	7	9.51	5	0
9	D Overhead Side Pass	-	3	-	x	2-3	**10**	8	9.6	5-10	1
10	Catch Cut Technique	x	1	-	x	1	**11**	2	10.0	5-10	1
11	Go Fetch It	x	1	-	x	1-2	**12**	10	10.1	2-10	0
12	Coming to the Ball	x	1	-	x	1-2	**13**	11	10.11	5-10	1
13	Jump to Ball	-	2	-	x	1-2	**14**	12	10.2	5-10	0
14	Loose Ball Lesson	x	2	-	x	3	**15**	13	10.3	2-5	0
15	Catching Bad Passes	x	1	-	x	2	**16**	14	10.4	2-5	0
16	Cut Fake Technique	x	2	-	-	1-2	**17**	none	10.5	5-10	0
17	Cut to the Ball	-	2	-	x	2-3	**18**	12,16	10.6	5-15	1
18	Three Second Lesson 1-2	-	1	x	-	1	**19**	17	10.7	3-4	1
19	Overplay the Catcher	-	3	x	x	3	**20**	8,17	10.8	5-20	3

1 Passing Technique

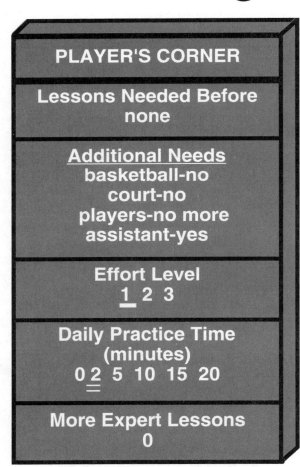

PLAYER'S CORNER

Lessons Needed Before
none

Additional Needs
basketball-no
court-no
players-no more
assistant-yes

Effort Level
<u>1</u> 2 3

Daily Practice Time (minutes)
0 <u>2</u> 5 10 15 20

More Expert Lessons
0

Brief:
Players flick their wrists with their arms in several passing positions.

Why Do This
The key to passing–like the key to shooting and dribbling–is the wrist flick. Players must flick passes with the arms outstretched from often awkward positions. Note that the chest pass, a part of basketball history, is infrequently used and then only when the defense is loose. For this reason it is not a separate lesson.

Directions
1. Start with your arms straight up overhead; elbows straight; palms facing forward.

2. Flick the wrists back and let them come forward naturally. Continue to do this while you follow the other directions.

3. Slowly move the arms to the right side keeping the elbows straight. The palms face forward. As the arms move down, bend the legs as well. Bend through the half down position. In the full down position the hands are inches from the ground.

Moving Through the Positions

up   half down   full down

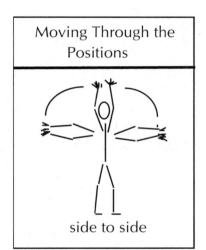

Moving Through the Positions

side to side

4. Continue flicking the wrists as you move. Move the arms back to the original position overhead.

5. Then move the arms to the left side as you bend the legs to the full down position.

6. Repeat this side to side arm movement while moving up and down several times.

Key Points

1. Make sure that the palms are always facing forward.

2. The wrists need to be flicked backward, not forward.

3. The fingers on the hand need to be spread apart, not closed, in a claw-like position.

4. It is difficult to flick the wrists with the arms on the sides as you bend and stretch. Throwing passes from this position is even more difficult.

2 Overhead Short Pass

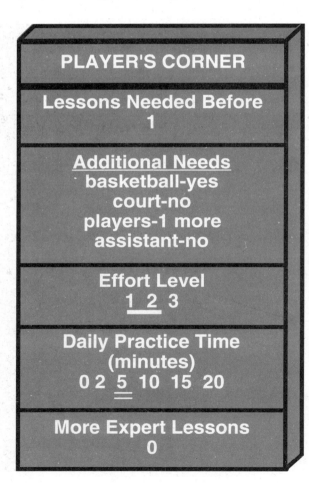

PLAYER'S CORNER

Lessons Needed Before
1

Additional Needs
basketball-yes
court-no
players-1 more
assistant-no

Effort Level
1 2 3

**Daily Practice Time
(minutes)**
0 2 5 10 15 20

More Expert Lessons
0

Brief:
Players flick short two-handed overhead passes back and forth.

Why Do This

Wrist motion is a key to passing. Telegraphing passes results when the arms are used without the wrists. Players must fully extend their arms to have the longest possible reach around the defense. Players also must look nearly straight ahead to cloak the direction of the pass. Good defense will read the eyes as well, so do not look in any particular direction. Overtly looking away or down often gives away the pass direction. Effective passers do not give the defense a chance to react.

Directions

1. Two players line up about 2 yards apart.

2. Start with the ball overhead, elbows straight, hands clawed. Only the fingertips touch the ball. The wrists are loose.

3. Bend the wrists back as far as possible. As a fake, flick without passing. Then flick the ball using the wrists without the arms. Flick chest high passes.

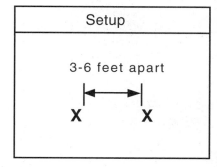

Setup
3-6 feet apart
X — X

4. Continue flicking the ball back and forth.

5. Half way through the lesson, switch pivot feet.

6. As wrists become stronger, move apart and throw harder passes.

Key Points

1. Do not use the arms.

2. After you catch the ball, move it overhead, keep elbows straight, wrists back, flick.

3. Do not look directly where you pass. Not looking in any particular direction is a difficult skill. It involves relaxing.

4. Initially, passes will be weak. Don't be dismayed, you will improve quickly.

5. The wrists stay loose.

6. Only the fingertips touch the ball.

3 Side Short Pass

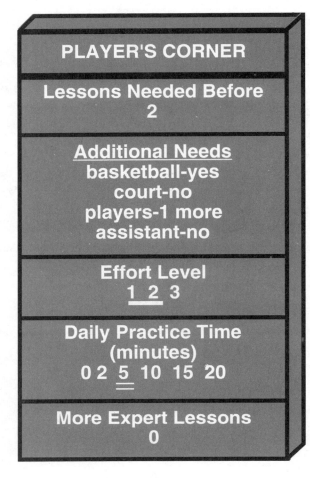

Brief:

Players flick short two-handed side passes back and forth.

Why Do This

With defense close, most passes start from a position other than overhead. Side passes are especially effective. However, they are the most difficult to execute.

Directions

1. Two players 2 yards apart face each other. One has the ball.

2. Position the arms directly to the side with the elbows as straight as possible. Palms face forward, not up.

3. Bend with the legs to the half down position. The back is nearly straight. This is an awkward position. It is even more difficult from the opposite side—left side for righties, right side for lefties. Older players can pass with one hand.

4. Start with the left foot as pivot foot.

5. Flick 5 passes from one side and then 5 from the other. Then switch pivot feet and repeat.

6. As wrists become stronger, move apart and throw harder passes.

Key Points

1. Do not use the arms.

2. The elbows are straight; wrists are back as far as possible; palms face forward.

3. Flick two-handed passes. This is difficult. Older players can use one hand.

4. Do not look in any particular direction.

5. Initially your passes will be weak. Don't worry; as you practice the technique, passes will be stronger.

Bounce Pass Positions

Throw 5 passes each way.

● pivot foot

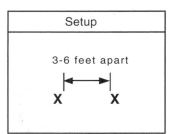

Setup

3-6 feet apart

X   X

4 Bounce Pass

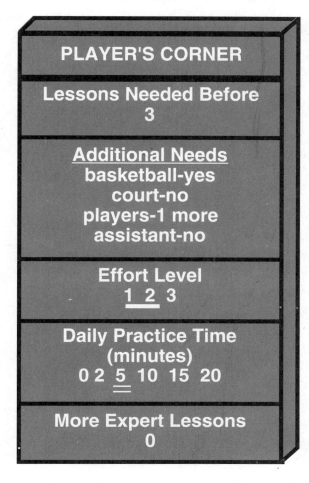

PLAYER'S CORNER

Lessons Needed Before
3

Additional Needs
basketball-yes
court-no
players-1 more
assistant-no

Effort Level
1 2 3

Daily Practice Time
(minutes)
0 2 5 10 15 20

More Expert Lessons
0

Brief:
Players flick short two-handed bounce passes back and forth.

Why Do This

Bounce passes are most effective in traffic especially when you are attempting to hit a player in the low post or lane. Bounce passes are also more difficult to intercept since their path is closer to the ground. However, they are slower to reach the catcher than regular passes and need to be thrown precisely. Effective bounce passes require more skill and practice than other types of passes.

The bounce pass in this lesson is a side bounce pass. There is no need to practice the chest bounce pass.

Directions

1. Two players face each other 2 yards apart.

2. The body is in the half down position so the ball can be released closer to the floor.

3. The elbows stay straight; just flick with the wrist. This is more difficult than the other passing lessons.

Bounce Pass Positions

Throw 5 passes each way.
● pivot foot

Bounce Passes

bounce 2/3^{rds} of
the way over
This pass is too high off the ground.

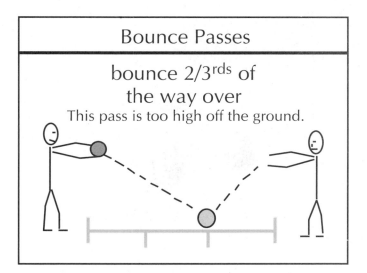

4. The pass bounces 2/3rds of the way, not half way, to the catcher. Aim at a mark or blemish on the floor that is at the proper distance or use a piece of masking tape.

5. The pass should be waist high or lower.

6. Flick 5 passes from one side and then 5 from the other. Then switch the pivot foot and repeat.

7. As wrists become stronger, move apart and throw harder passes.

Key Points

1. Do not use the arms.

2. The elbows are straight; wrists are back as far as possible; palms face forward.

3. The hand is clawed with only the fingertips touching the ball.

4. Flick two-handed passes. This is difficult. Older players can use one hand.

5. Do not look in any particular direction.

6. Initially, passes will be weak.

7. The pass bounces 2/3rds of the way to the catcher.

8. The bounce pass does not bounce high.

5 Baseball Pass

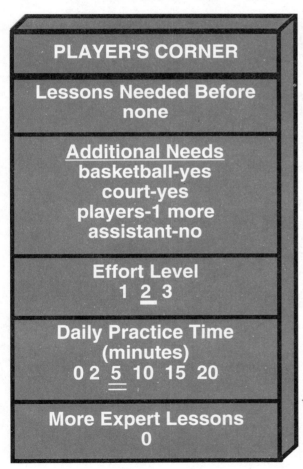

PLAYER'S CORNER

Lessons Needed Before
none

Additional Needs
basketball-yes
court-yes
players-1 more
assistant-no

Effort Level
1 <u>2</u> 3

Daily Practice Time
(minutes)
0 2 <u>5</u> 10 15 20

More Expert Lessons
0

Brief:

Players stand on opposite side-lines firing one-handed baseball passes back and forth. Novices initially stand closer.

Why Do This

The one-handed baseball pass is more important than you think. You need it for:

1) a long outlet pass after a rebound or

2) a long pass to a free player down court or

3) a long out-of-bounds pass during a press.

The baseball pass is the best way for a youngster, in particular, to throw a long pass because long two-handed passes require more strength.

Directions

1. Two players set up facing each other on opposite sidelines. Novices move closer initially.

2. Throw a one-armed pass to your partner on the other side of the court. Try not to maim any of your teammates with errant passes.

3. Don't worry about walking initially.

4. When you are more expert, pass alternating the pivot foot.

6 Baseball Pass Cut

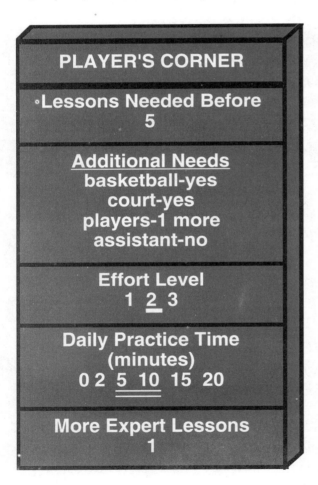

PLAYER'S CORNER

Lessons Needed Before
5

Additional Needs
basketball-yes
court-yes
players-1 more
assistant-no

Effort Level
1 <u>2</u> 3

Daily Practice Time (minutes)
0 2 <u>5 10</u> 15 20

More Expert Lessons
1

Brief:

One player throws a half court baseball pass to another player cutting to the basket.

Why Do This

This baseball pass lesson involves cutting, catching, communication, dribbling, and shooting as well. Using three players can create a continuous motion lesson. It is great lesson for youngsters because it develops both timing and the concept of timing. To keep things simple do it initially without shooting.

Directions

1. One player with the ball starts at the midcourt center jump circle.

2. The cutter starts on the right sideline halfway between the end and midcourt lines.

3. As soon as the passer controls the ball, make eye contact with the cutter. This signals the cut.

4. The cutter runs down the sideline. A few yards before the endline, fake by taking one step outside and then cut inward toward the basket. This is like the move an end on a football team makes.

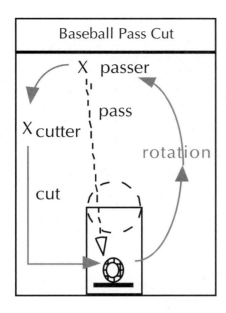

Baseball Pass Cut

X passer

pass

X cutter

cut

rotation

5. Time the baseball pass so that the cutter and the ball meet at the basket.

6. At the basket catch the ball and then come to a complete stop. Initially do not shoot. Three players can rotate around the court to the next position.

7. Throw a baseball pass back to the passer and return to the starting position. Halfway through the lesson, cut from on the other sideline.

Key Points

1. The pass and the cutter meet at the basket.

2. After a quick cut, a one foot shot is taken without hurry.

3. Players make eye contact before the cut. This is not a 10 minute look.

4. The cutter takes a step outward before cutting inward toward the basket.

More Expert Lessons

Baseball Pass Catch with Shot

Add shooting. Stop after catching the ball at the basket. Take a one foot shot, not a layup. Rebound your shot. Baseball pass back to midcourt.

7 Pivot Pass

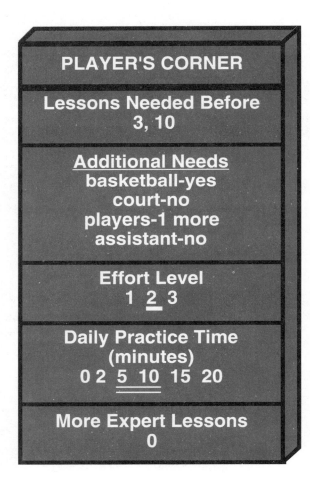

PLAYER'S CORNER

Lessons Needed Before
3, 10

Additional Needs
basketball-yes
court-no
players-1 more
assistant-no

Effort Level
1 **2** 3

Daily Practice Time (minutes)
0 2 **5 10** 15 20

More Expert Lessons
0

Brief:
Players catch, pivot, and then pass.

Why Do This

Pivoting to pass is probably the most commonly used move in basketball. Players execute it nearly every time they take possession of the ball. Note that you need to learn the basic catching technique from Lesson 10 first.

Directions

1. Two players face each other 4-6 yards apart.

2. Start with the ball in the overhead position, elbows straight, wrists bent back as far as possible. The left foot is the pivot foot.

3. Flick an overhead pass.

4. Catch the ball using the left foot as the pivot foot. Do not catch the ball and then switch pivot feet. Forward pivot around once with the ball overhead before passing.

5. After every five passes, alternate the pivot foot.

6. Switch the type of pass thrown every 1-2 minutes or 20 passes. Start with the overhead, then do the side and bounce passes.

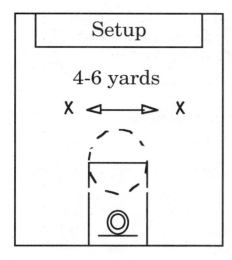

Setup

4-6 yards

X ◁——▷ X

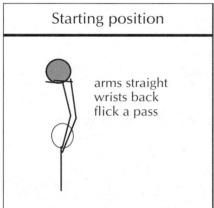

Starting position

arms straight
wrists back
flick a pass

Key Points

1. Flick passes without using the arms.

2. Prepare to catch the ball on the proper pivot foot.

3. Players tend to use a favorite pivot foot, so make sure to switch after 5 passes.

More Expert Lessons

Fake Pass Plus

Add or repeat this passing lesson using a flick fake as you pivot. Pivot around in the backward direction as well. Make sure to switch pivot feet.

8 Pass Communication 1-2

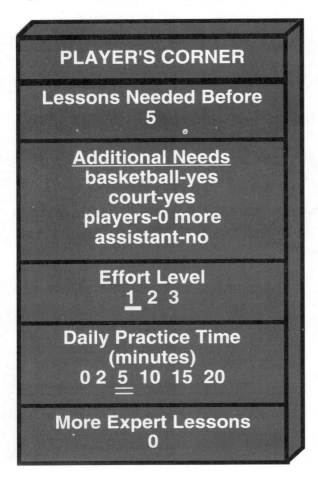

PLAYER'S CORNER

Lessons Needed Before
5

Additional Needs
basketball-yes
court-yes
players-0 more
assistant-no

Effort Level
<u>1</u> 2 3

Daily Practice Time (minutes)
0 2 <u>5</u> 10 15 20

More Expert Lessons
0

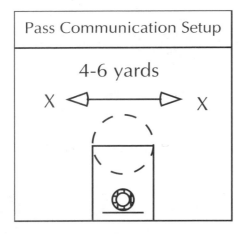

Pass Communication Setup

4-6 yards

X ⟵⟶ X

Brief:
Players catch, pivot, and then pass in groups of two.

Why Do This

A key to successful passing in a game is nonverbal communication. Passers need to let catchers know where to cut. Catchers in turn must let passers know where and when they will cut. In this lesson players communicate in two ways before making the pass. Initially don't worry about being too overt–you need to communicate. With practice and experience, communication becomes more subtle.

In **Part 1** the catcher uses these two methods:

   1) The catcher positions the arms and hands where he wants the ball thrown. This is like a baseball catcher making a pocket for the pitcher to aim at. The hands can be placed anywhere–to the side, high, low, to the back, forward.

   2) Point with the hand, eyes, or the nose in the direction that the catcher wants to move to catch the ball. Besides left and right, the ball can be passed forward or toward the back.

In **Part 2** the passer uses these similar methods:

   1) Point with the hand or the ball in the direction that you want to throw the pass; the catcher must move in this direction.

   2) Point with the head, eyes, or the nose in the direction that you want the catcher to go.

Directions

Part 1

1. Two players set up 4-6 yards apart. Repeat any passing lesson–Lesson 2 is easiest–with the catcher communicating to the passer where to throw the ball. Communicate as described above.

2. Change the type of communication frequently.

3. Vary the type of pass and pivot foot used to pass as well. Execute 5 each way. You can catch the ball on either foot.

Part 2

4. The passer does the directing in this lesson. Use the two methods described above.

Key Points

1. Players flick passes without using the arms.

2. It is okay if communication is obvious at first.

3. Switch pivot feet and the type of pass frequently- every 5 passes.

4. Initially let the catcher communicate to the passer. Reverse this in Part 2.

5. It is okay to discuss things between passes and invent signals. You can tell the other player that scratching your nose means to go back for a high pass. Any system is okay–just communicate.

9 D Overhead Side Pass

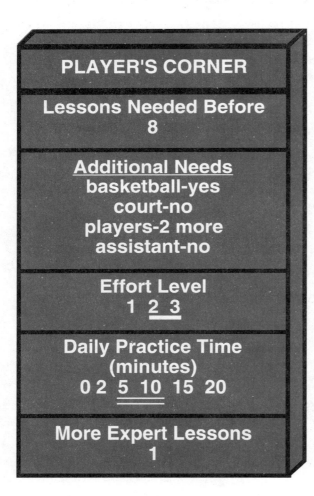

Brief:

A player makes an overhead or side pass with defense covering him or her.

Why Do This

Passing with the defense right in your face is difficult. However, this is how it is in a game. Passing must be practiced this way after the basic techniques are learned. In this lesson the defense covers the passer, not the catcher. The catcher and passer communicate as they did in Lesson 8. Since the defense moves directly from one passer to the other, this is a hustle lesson as well. Don't make this "Monkey in the Middle"–when the catcher pivots around, the defense must hustle to set up on the other passer.

Directions

1. The passer and the catcher are 3-6 yards apart.

2. The defense sets up one foot from the passer. Attempt to block the pass and the vision of the passer. Slowly count out loud to 5 to start and end the play. After a pass, hustle to cover the other passer. The defense increases aggressiveness as the offense improves.

Overhead Side Pass in Steps

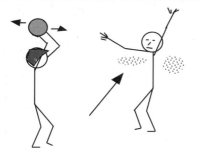

Ball and step fake to either side then push the ball past the defense under the arm pits.

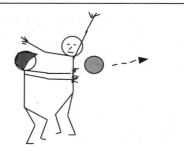

Release the ball when it is past the body and arm of the defense.

3. The passer has five seconds to get the pass off. Use either an overhead or side pass initially, no bounce passes. Alternate pivot foot.

4. The catcher communicates to the passer where to pass the ball. After catching the ball, pivot around once and then pass. The pivoting gives the defense time to set up on you.

6. The defense immediately runs to the other passer and starts counting again. This looks a little like "Monkey in the Middle."

7. An offensive player should rotate to defense after every 5 passes.

8. Tips for the passer:

　a. Do not wait for the defense.

　b. Pivot with the ball in a position to pass.

　c. Move the ball constantly from side to side.

　d. Use ball and step fakes. These are described in detail in The Player's Bible—Lessons 12, 16-18.

　e. Move the ball and your arms beyond the body and hands of the defense before you let the ball go. This move prevents the defense from stopping the pass.

　f. Fake high and then push the ball under the outstretched arm of the defense.

Key Points

1. You may have great difficulty with this lesson because many skills are applied. This is why the defense starts off at less than full intensity.

2. The defense does not flail their arms at the ball.

3. Players tend to use the same pivot foot each time. This severely hampers their ability to execute skills in a game. Make sure you regularly switch.

4. Fake and move the ball a lot.

5. The defense must hustle to the other passer after each pass.

More Expert Lessons

Defense Bounce Pass

Repeat this lesson using bounce passes. Fake high and then push the ball down and past the outstretched hands and body of the defense. Releasing the ball beyond the defense makes it difficult for the defense to interfere with the pass.

10 Catch Cut Technique

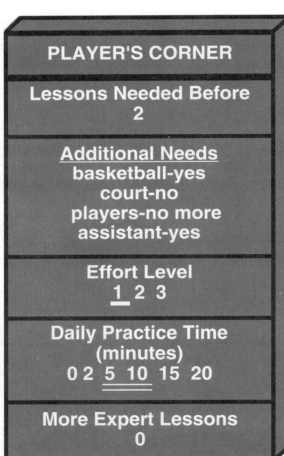

PLAYER'S CORNER

Lessons Needed Before
2

Additional Needs
basketball-yes
court-no
players-no more
assistant-yes

Effort Level
1 2 3

Daily Practice Time
(minutes)
0 2 5 10 15 20

More Expert Lessons
0

Brief:
Players jump toward the ball with outstretched arms and hands just before it reaches them.

Why Do This
Catching a ball is not as simple as it looks. You jump just before catching the ball so that you can rearrange your steps to land balanced without walking. The position of the hands and arms is important as well. Spread the fingers apart to make the hand claw-like. Fully outstretch the arms in the direction of the pass. Novices will have difficulty.

Directions
1. Set up 5 feet away from the assistant.

2. Stand with the right foot forward, hands clawed, and arms outstretched.

3. In this position jump just before you catch the ball. Catch the ball while in the air. Land on the back foot, the pivot foot, first.

4. The jump is just high enough to arrange or rearrange your feet after you catch the ball.

5. Repeat 5-10 times and then do this lesson with the left foot forward.

Catching the Ball from a Standing Position

| ready to catch | jump up | catch in air | land on back foot | stop |

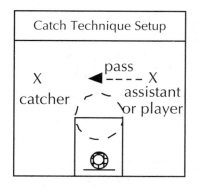

Catch Technique Setup

X
catcher
pass
X
assistant
or player

Key Points

1. The hands are clawed in a ready position to catch the ball. The arms are fully extended.

2. The jump should take place when the ball is almost in the hands.

3. Novices will have difficulty initially. After two or three practices they will catch the ball more naturally.

More Expert Lessons

Catching Technique 2

Repeat this lesson catching the ball on the front foot and stepping forward with the back foot. You jump, catch, land on the front foot and move the back foot forward while in the air. This extra step slows you down after catching a pass on the run. Do this lesson with an assistant and then, when more expert, flick the ball to another player. Make sure to switch the pivot foot after every 5 catches.

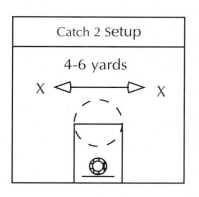

Catch 2 Setup

4-6 yards

X ⟵⟶ X

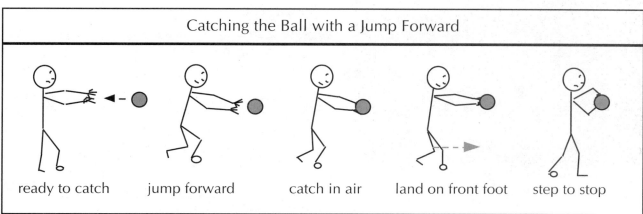

Catching the Ball with a Jump Forward

| ready to catch | jump forward | catch in air | land on front foot | step to stop |

11 Go Fetch It

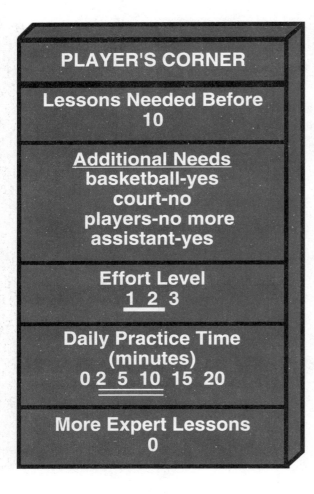

Brief:

Players run after a ball thrown in a direction away from them, pick it up, pivot, and pass.

Why Do This

This lesson is a diagnostic test for catching without walking. You hustle after the ball and slow down after you grab it. Doing this slowly improves your balance and footwork. It is very worthwhile for novices.

Directions

1. Stand 5 yards away from the assistant who has the ball.

2. The assistant throws a grounder 5 yards to the left or right of your position. Increase the speed of this pass as the catcher becomes more expert.

3. Go after the ball, grab it, and then slow down.

4. Pivot around and throw it back to the assistant. Go back to the original position.

5. The "hitch" is how you pick up the ball. Just before picking it up, jump slightly to arrange your feet properly as in Lesson 10.

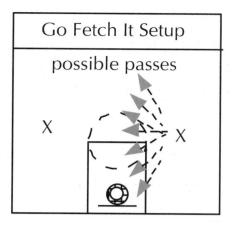

Go Fetch It Setup

possible passes

X   X

6. Say, "Jump, grab, one, two" (or just "jump, one, two") when you pick up the ball. The one is a step on the pivot foot. The two is a step to stop.

Key Points

1. This lesson is for novices of all degrees so the velocity of the ball, how far away it is tossed, and the speed the catcher needs to run "to fetch it" should be varied accordingly.

2. Slow down only after the ball is grabbed, not before. Many players slow down to catch the ball.

3. Players often have trouble with the "one, two." If you take these 2 steps like a player on a tight rope (ready to fall off) just take a few extra steps; count "1,2,3" or "1,2,3,4" so you do not lose balance. Don't worry about walking. When you have balance you will be able to stop in 2 steps. Note that you probably need more practice of Lesson 10.

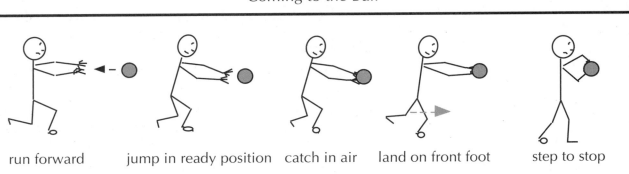

run forward   jump in ready position   catch in air   land on front foot   step to stop

12 Coming to the Ball

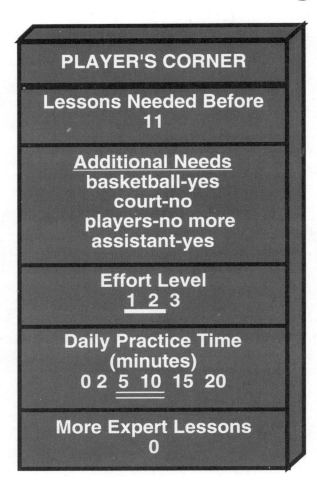

PLAYER'S CORNER

Lessons Needed Before
11

Additional Needs
basketball-yes
court-no
players-no more
assistant-yes

Effort Level
1 2 3

Daily Practice Time
(minutes)
0 2 5 10 15 20

More Expert Lessons
0

Brief:

A player runs directly toward the ball, without stopping until after catching it.

Why Do This

Coming to the ball is the key to catching the ball. Otherwise, the defense comes to the ball ahead of the offense and catches it.

Directions

1. The player sets up 5-10 yards from the assistant who has the ball.

2. The player runs toward the assistant as the assistant throws or rolls the ball directly toward the player.

3. Initially, players run slowly to the ball. Eventually they sprint to the ball.

4. Players jump to arrange their feet just before grabbing the ball. Players say, "jump, grab, one, two" or just, "jump, one, two" as they catch the ball.

5. Players must grab the ball and then slow down. Make sure not to slow down before the grab.

6. Since players are running toward the ball, the first foot down after the catch is the pivot foot. The second foot is the stop. Note that some novices may need a third and fourth step to slow down initially. This is okay. It may take a day or two to stop balanced.

Key Points

1. Run to the ball without slowing down or stopping until after catching it.

2. Take a few extra steps after the catch or run at a slower speed, if the player is off-balance on the catch. The initial purpose of this lesson is getting balanced on the catch.

3. Increase the speed of each run as the player becomes more expert. Eventually the player should sprint to the ball.

4. This lesson is a key to team offense against tight defenses.

More Expert Lessons

Sprint to the Ball

Players have a tendency to slow down before catching a pass, instead of after catching a pass. This lesson is a good cure for folks who slow down.

1. The player should start 10 yards from the assistant.

2. Instead of sprinting directly toward the assistant, the player should run 2-5 yards to one side or the other.

3. On each run the assistant should release the pass at different times:

a. after the sprinter has run 3 yards.

b. after 7 yards.

c. when the sprinter goes right by.

d. when the sprinter has run 5-10 yards past the assistant.

This last run is the most important one, because players have a tendency to slow down. Repeat this last pass several times in a row, until the player continues at full speed before the catch.

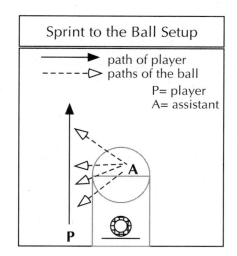

Sprint to the Ball Setup

→ path of player
----▷ paths of the ball
P= player
A= assistant

13 Jump to the Ball

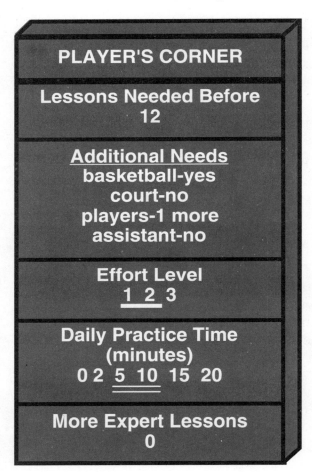

PLAYER'S CORNER

Lessons Needed Before
12

Additional Needs
basketball-yes
court-no
players-1 more
assistant-no

Effort Level
1 <u>2</u> 3

Daily Practice Time
(minutes)
0 2 <u>5 10</u> 15 20

More Expert Lessons
0

Brief:

A player long jumps to the ball as he catches it.

Why Do This

In this last step before catching the ball a player long jumps forward toward the ball. This prevents the defense from jumping in front to interfere with the pass. This is exactly what you do in the low post area when you want to catch a pass in the lane. The passer and the catcher must communicate so that the jump forward and the pass are timed properly.

Directions

1. Two players line up about 5 yards apart ready to throw overhead passes back and forth.

2. The passer fakes an overhead pass and then throws one.

3. The catcher stands sideways. The foot closer to the ball is the starting pivot foot.

4. The fake signals the catcher to pivot around forward. Move the back foot ahead of the pivot foot; then long jump forward toward the passer as far as possible with arms outstretched and fingers spread.

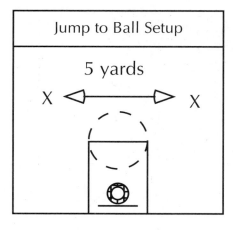

Jump to Ball Setup

5 yards

X ⟵⟶ X

5. Catch the ball before landing. Either foot can be the pivot on the catch.

6. The passer and catcher need to work out the timing.

7. The catcher alternates the side he or she faces before jumping forward. The passer alternates the pivot foot.

Key Points

1. The catcher makes a pocket or target for the passer with the hands.

2. The jump forward is a long jump not a high jump.

3. The catcher has outstretched arms with fingers spread, ready to catch the ball.

4. The catcher switches the side she faces and the passer switches the pivot foot after each pass.

5. It may be easier to use the back foot as the pivot after you catch the ball. Do whatever is easiest—don't walk.

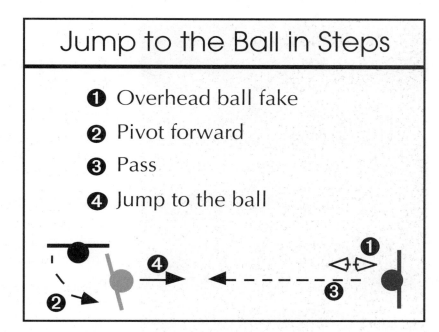

Jump to the Ball in Steps

❶ Overhead ball fake

❷ Pivot forward

❸ Pass

❹ Jump to the ball

14 Loose Ball Lesson

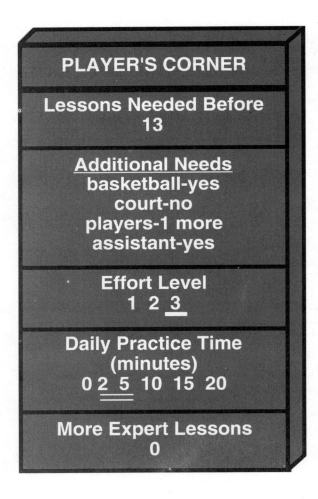

PLAYER'S CORNER

Lessons Needed Before
13

Additional Needs
basketball-yes
court-no
players-1 more
assistant-yes

Effort Level
1 2 <u>3</u>

**Daily Practice Time
(minutes)**
0 <u>2</u> <u>5</u> 10 15 20

More Expert Lessons
0

Brief:
Two players go for a loose ball.

Why Do This

The key to retrieving a loose ball is to prevent the other player from getting there first. Step in front and then go for the ball. This is similar to actions taken to rebound.

Directions

1. Two players line up, side to side, elbow to elbow, leaning against each other. Place the ball 2 feet away.

2. The assistant yells *go*.

3. Step in front of the other player. Attempt to push your foot and arm first, and then your body in front of them. This is called *getting position*.

4. Get position first, then go for the ball. Stop after one player gets the ball.

5. After repeating this 5-10 times, the assistant tosses the ball slowly in any direction, even toward the players, instead of just placing it on the floor.

6. Players go for it as they did when the ball was stationary.

15 Catching Bad Passes

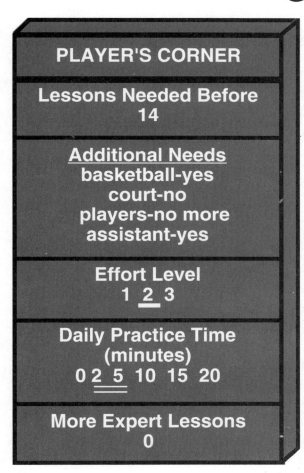

PLAYER'S CORNER

Lessons Needed Before
14

Additional Needs
basketball-yes
court-no
players-no more
assistant-yes

Effort Level
1 <u>2</u> 3

Daily Practice Time (minutes)
0 <u>2</u> <u>5</u> 10 15 20

More Expert Lessons
0

Brief:
Players catch intentionally thrown bad passes.

Why Do This

Players often receive passes that are off the mark or timed improperly during a game. There are many reasons for this. Defenses are tight. Other defensive players can deflect the ball. A simple miscue. In any case this is a poor excuse to let the pass go. Each player needs to go after bad passes. This lesson teaches a player how to catch a bad pass as well as emphasizes the need to go after it.

Directions

1. Set up 4-6 yards away from an assistant.

2. When you jump forward for a pass, the assistant will throw you a bad one. Catch it or at least stop it.

3. Initially the assistant throws passes that bounce right in front of the player. Then the assistant throws passes that are off to one side. The speed of the passes depends on the level of the player. Usually only slow to medium speed passes are needed.

16 Cut Fake Technique

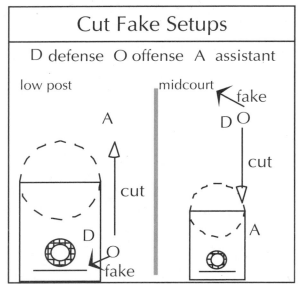

Cut Fake Setups

D defense O offense A assistant

low post   midcourt

Brief:
Before cutting, a player makes one of several fakes.

Why Do This
Faking without the ball is a skill that is often overlooked by coaches. Cutting and faking go hand in hand. It is difficult to think of a situation where faking before cutting is not essential. Several fakes are often used together or one right after the other. In each case the fake only needs to slow down the defense by one step. This enables the offense to be open for an instant. Faking a cut, on the other hand, is used to keep the defense close. This allows other players to operate more freely.

Directions
1. Two players line up next to each other either at the low post or near midcourt. The defense stays put. The assistant watches from a distance.

The Sleep Fake
2. The first fake is one that is accomplished only too readily. It is the sleep fake. Relax. Appear to be uninvolved. Turn away from the action slowly. Actually, pay close attention to everything. You are waiting for the right instant to cut.

3. Do this fake while the assistant talks to you. When he holds up three fingers, sprint forward toward the assistant.

4. The assistant does not make it easy to see her fingers. Hold up 2 and then 4, as many times as needed before holding up 3.

5. The assistant needs to watch the player's fake and inform the player whether or not the fake is convincing.

The Step Away Fake

6. The step away fake works well with the sleep fake. Take several lazy steps in the opposite direction that you plan to cut.

The Step Behind Fake

7. The best fake involves sleepily stepping behind the defense; step between the defense and the basket. Step away just far enough that the defense is out of touching range. You want the defense to forget about you. In any case, they cannot see you and the ball at the same time. This works best against zones.

8. The defense starts in the half down defensive position facing the assistant. Do not move. In a game, this is not the way to play defense. You never let players walk behind you without blocking their path as well as staying in contact by touch.

9. When the defense turns to look, sprint toward the assistant. Again, in a game the defense never turns around.

Key Points

1. Make sure players look like they are sleeping.

2. The fakes are very slow, whereas the cuts are sprints. The cut is like the start of a 50 yard dash.

3. Players have a tendency to fake too quickly and sprint too slowly.

4. In this lesson the defense stands around. However, the defense needs to learn how to cover players who fake. See the defensive overplaying lessons.

17 Cut to the Ball

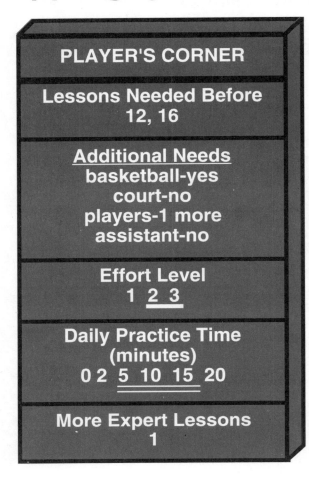

PLAYER'S CORNER

Lessons Needed Before
12, 16

Additional Needs
basketball-yes
court-no
players-1 more
assistant-no

Effort Level
1 **2 3**

Daily Practice Time
(minutes)
0 2 **5 10 15** 20

More Expert Lessons
1

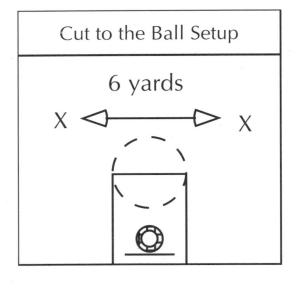

Cut to the Ball Setup

6 yards

X ←——→ X

Brief:
Players fake and then cut to the ball.

Why Do This

To catch a pass you cut either to the ball or to the open space. In this lesson you cut directly forward to the ball after communication with the passer. Presses, especially full court presses, can readily be beaten when players possess this skill. This lesson is of particular importance to novices and their coaches. Do this lesson at the practice level before speeding up.

Directions

1. Players set up about 6 yards apart.

2. The catcher fakes and then cuts to the ball. Use the step away sleep fake.

3. Stop running only after you catch the ball. Think- *jump, catch, one, two*. Stop on the one, two.

4. The passer throws the ball after the fake at the start of the actual cut. Use an overhead pass.

5. Repeat this, switching roles. Alternate the pivot foot in each role. Use side and side bounce passes as well.

Key Points

1. The catcher catches the ball, takes two steps (this is considered $1^1/_2$ steps), and then stops.

2. Catchers have the arms outstretched, hands ready, and fingers spread as they cut.

3. It is important to alternate the pivot foot when both catching and passing.

4. Players not ready for this lesson have a tendency to stop before they catch the ball. If this is the case work on a Lesson 12, Coming to the Ball.

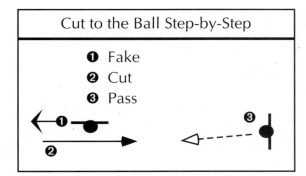

Cut to the Ball Step-by-Step

❶ Fake
❷ Cut
❸ Pass

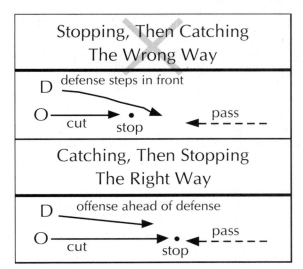

**Stopping, Then Catching
The Wrong Way**

D defense steps in front
O — cut → · stop → ← pass

**Catching, Then Stopping
The Right Way**

D offense ahead of defense
O — cut → · ← pass
        stop

More Expert Lessons

Cut Communication

Repeat this lesson with the passer and catcher deciding on two things before each pass.

1. The signal to start.

The passer usually gives the signal. A look or a ball fake are commonly used signals. Cutters often use a fake as a signal.

2. Where the ball and the catcher will meet.

The ball can be thrown short—even a lateral is okay—or long to one side or another. The defense often determines this, but in this lesson the offensive players do. Passers nonchalantly point with a finger or other body part in the direction they want cutters to go.

Initially players discuss what signals to use. Eventually they intuitively respond to each other.

18 Three Second Lesson 1-2

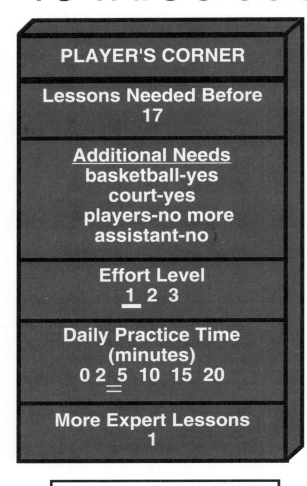

PLAYER'S CORNER

Lessons Needed Before
17

Additional Needs
basketball-yes
court-yes
players-no more
assistant-no

Effort Level
__1__ 2 3

**Daily Practice Time
(minutes)**
0 2 __5__ 10 15 20

More Expert Lessons
1

Setup

Parts 1 and 2

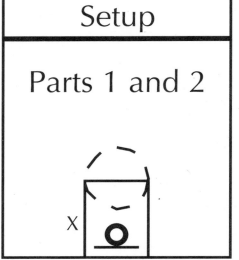

Brief:
You cut into the lane and stay there for the maximum amount of time before getting out.

Why Do This

Often novice players go into the lane on offense without counting. The result is 3-second violations. This lesson teaches you to count as well as jump into the lane for a pass. This only needs to be done a few times. There are two parts to this lesson.

Directions

Part 1

1. Line up on either side of the lane in the low post. Do not stand on the line.

2. Start counting when you step into the lane. Count out loud—one one thousand, two one thousand, out. As you say "out," step out of the lane.

3. Repeat this 10 times.

Part 2

4. Jump into the lane ready to catch a pass. The arms are outstretched and the body is in the half down ready position. Count as you did before. Jump out of the lane.

5. Repeat this 10 times.

Key Points

1. For Part 2, players jump into the lane ready to catch the ball.

2. If the ball arrives after the jump, you must jump and move to the ball again, not just wait for the ball to arrive.

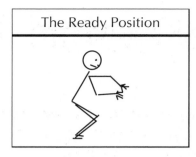

The Ready Position

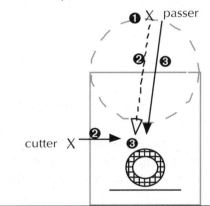

Cut into Lane Step-by-Step

❶ passer fakes

❷ cutter jumps into lane
passer passes

❸ cutter catches ball and shoots
passer follows ball to basket

cutter

More Expert Lessons

Cut Into Lane

This is like Part 2 above except that each player receives a pass in the lane, then turns to the basket, and shoots. The passer starts at the top of the key.

Directions

1. The overhead fake by the passer is the signal to the low post player to jump into the lane. Throw an overhead pass so that the player and the ball meet at the basket.

2. The cutter catches the ball, pivots, shoots, and rebounds.

3. The passer follows the ball to the basket for the rebound, then goes to the low post position.

4. Halfway through the lesson switch the cutting position to the other side of the basket.

5. Repeat using side or bounce passes.

19 Overplay the Catcher

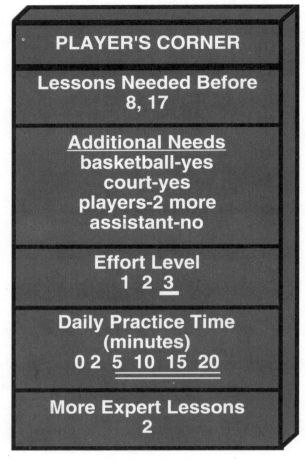

PLAYER'S CORNER

Lessons Needed Before
8, 17

Additional Needs
basketball-yes
court-yes
players-2 more
assistant-no

Effort Level
1 2 <u>3</u>

**Daily Practice Time
(minutes)**
0 2 <u>5 10 15 20</u>

More Expert Lessons
2

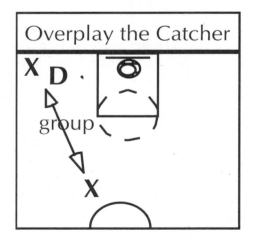

Overplay the Catcher

X D

group

X

Brief:
The catcher catches a pass while being overplayed by the defense.

Why Do This
At last, the first realistic passing and catching lesson. You think you can pass and catch! Wait till you do this. In a game your team has a big lead, then the defense full court presses you to smithereens. Guess what! You need practice. By now you know the techniques. Expect to have problems with this lesson. If a pass makes it to the catcher, you may have cause to celebrate. This is extremely difficult. However, the reward are commensurate with the difficulty.

Note that the defense needs to know how to overplay to make this lesson worthwhile. Do the defensive lessons first. In brief, overplaying involves staying on one side of the offense with one foot ahead. Shoulder to shoulder your body points to the ball. Watch the ball. Play the offense by touch. One hand is outstretched forward to block any pass.

Directions

1. Two offensive players set up 7 yards apart. The defense overplays the catcher. Use a small area, no larger than 7 X 7 yards, for this lesson. See the setup diagram.

2. The passer signals the start of the lesson by faking an overhead pass. Then count slowly and loudly to five.

3. If the ball is not passed by the count of five, the lesson ends.

4. Rotate positions from passer to catcher to defense and repeat.

5. Halfway through the lesson (or every other time), the defense overplays from the other side of the offense.

Position Rotation

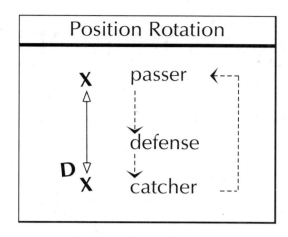

D on Catcher Cut without Defense

Step 1—A cuts to **B** for a pass

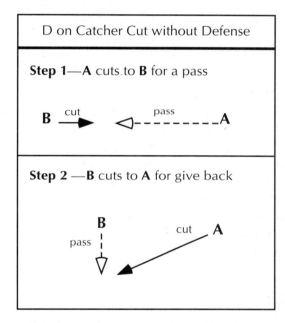

Step 2 —B cuts to **A** for give back

Setup

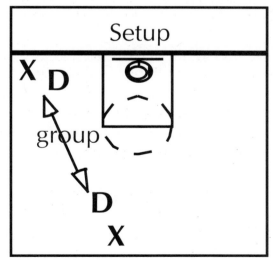

Key Points

1. Go back to previous lessons if needed and most certainly do the defensive overplay lessons first.

2. Communicate with the other players.

3. Use fakes.

4. Come to the ball.

5. Stay within the small area designated for this lesson. This makes it more difficult.

6. The pass and the catcher meet at a point.

7. No dribbling allowed.

More Expert Lessons

Front The Catcher

The defense fronts, instead of overplaying, the catcher. Fronting involves facing up to the defense without watching the passer. It is used in presses and out-of-bounds plays. The defense moves with the midsection of the offense and watches the eyes for telltale signs of a pass. Do the defensive fronting lessons first.

D On Catcher, Cut

After the pass, with the defense either overplaying or fronting, the passer cuts to the ball. The defense endeavors to obstruct the pass back. This is a *give and go* (pass and cut to the ball) play for the passer.

D Pass, Overplay Catcher

1. Setup–The same as the main lesson with the addition of a defensive player on the passer. Position the initial passer toward the center of the court. The initial catchers are toward the out-of-bounds lines. Play toward the out-of-bounds lines. The defense sets up to overplay the catcher.

2. The passer signals the cut. The cutter fakes, then cuts to a spot or the ball. Communicate to decide.

3. Try each lesson twice without changing positions. The first switch involves the offense and defense. The next involves the initial catching and passing positions.

4. To start the lesson the defense loudly counts to five when the passer has the ball. If the pass is not made by five the play ends. Unsuccessful tries count.

we've got videos and clinics

THE BASKETBALL COACH'S BIBLE WILL HELP YOU BY ...

✦ showing you how best to plan and run practice
✦ supplying two hundred field tested lessons ready to use
✦ systematically teaching each skill, step-by-step
✦ not skipping basic steps essential to your success
✦ presenting strategies, a warm down, game statistics and more
✦ saving you time by giving you methods and ideas that work

books

A. **The Basketball Coach's Bible**   350 pages
   Everything about coaching. (07-5) $24.95
B. **The Basketball Player's Bible**   270 pages
   All individual fundamentals. (13-X) $19.95
C. **The Basketball Shooting Guide** 45 pages
   Yields permanent improvement. (14-8) $ 6.95
D. **The Basketball Scoring Guide**   47 pages
   Teaches pro moves step-by-step. (15-6) $ 6.95
E. **The Basketball Dribbling Guide** 46 pages
   Anyone can be a good dribbler. (16-4) $ 6.95
F. **The Basketball Defense Guide**   46 pages
   Defense in every situation. (17-2) $ 6.95
G. **The Basketball Pass Cut Catch Guide** 47 pages
   Be an effective team player. (18-0) $ 6.95
H. **Basketball Fundamentals**   46 pages
   Covers all fundamentals. (08-3) $ 6.95
I. **Planning Basketball Practice**   46 pages
   Use time effectively, plan, plus. (09-1) $ 6.95
J. 9 **Book Series**, A - I (01-6)   ~$20 off $ 81.50 w/ship
K. 2 **Book Bible Set**, A,B (20-2)   ~$5 off $ 46.13 w/ship
L. 7 **Guide Set**, C - I (21-0)   ~ $5 off $ 49.50 w/ship

videos
40-60 MINUTES; $24.95 EACH
CHECK FOR AVAILABILITY

1. **Fundamentals I** Over 25 individual skill topics. (77-6)
2. **Fundamentals II** Team Skills, plays & pressure defense (90-3)
3. **Planning Practice I** Daily, weekly, and seasonal planning. (75-X)
4. **Planning Practice II** Get 5 times more out of practice. (76-8)
5. **Shooting I** Technique, Hook, Jump Shot & Layup (78-4)
6. **Shooting II** Foul Shooting, 3-Point Shooting, Driving (79-2)
7. **Shooting III** Shooting under pressure, Scoring Moves, Faking (80-6)
8. **Dribbling** Technique, Position, Protect Ball, Looking Up (81-4)
9. **Defense I** Position, Forcing, Trapping, On Shooter (84-9)
10. **Defense II** lane/Post, overplay, Front, Help, Strong-Weak (85-7)
11. **Passing I** Technique, Overhead, Bounce, Communication (82-2)
12. **Passing II** Cutting, Faking, Passing with Defense (83-0)
13. **Rebounding/Picking** Going for the Ball, Positioning, Boxing out (91-1)
14. **The Transition Game** from Foul Line, Center Jump & Plays (86-5)
15. **Team Offense** Offensive setup, Plays, Pliable Offense (87-3)
16. **Team Defense** Helping Out, Zone Shift, Half Court Trap (88-1)
17. **Full Court Pressure** Offense, Trapping Zone, Out-of-Bounds (89-X)

SIDNEY GOLDSTEIN, MR. BASKETBALL BASICS, TELLS YOU ABOUT HIS BOOKS

"This series is about fundamentals. It is a step back to the basics and a step forward to improved training methods. It is a place to start and to return again and again. No matter what your coaching level, age or sex the fundamentals do not change. You will reap great rewards by recognizing, practicing, and applying them to your situation. Visit our web site for 60 pages of information about our books, more comments from coaches, reviews, discounts, freebies, basketball articles, tips, videos, clinics, and more: I guarantee satisfaction."

clinics

VISIT OUR WEB SITE FOR DATE, TIME, AND LOCATION OF COACH AND PLAYER CLINICS:
www.mrbasketball.net

order form

QTY	ITEM	TITLE	PRICE

SHIPPING
$25 = $5; $50 = $5.75; $75 = $6.50
ADD $1 FOR HOME DELIVERY

DISCOUNTS 50-75%
CALL OR CHECK
www.mrbasketball.net

SUBTOTAL _____
ADD 7% SALES TAX IN PA _____
SHIPPING _____
TOTAL ORDER _____

ALL BOOKS ARE 8.5x11. ALL GUIDES COST 6.95; NEW EDITIONS COST **$7.45** WHEN AVAILABLE. ALL VIDEOS COST $24.95 EACH AND RUN 45-60 MINUTES. ISBN 1-884357-(XX-X) SUFFIX IN PARENTHESIS

HOW TO ORDER
Call **1-800-979-8642**
Use our web site: **www.mrbasketball.net**
Fax PO's to: **215-438-4459**

Use your credit card, send a money order or PO to:
**Golden Aura Publishing
P.O. Box 41012
Phila., PA 19127-1012**

name _____
address _____
city _____ state_____ zip_____
phone _____
card # _____ exp_____ home zip_____